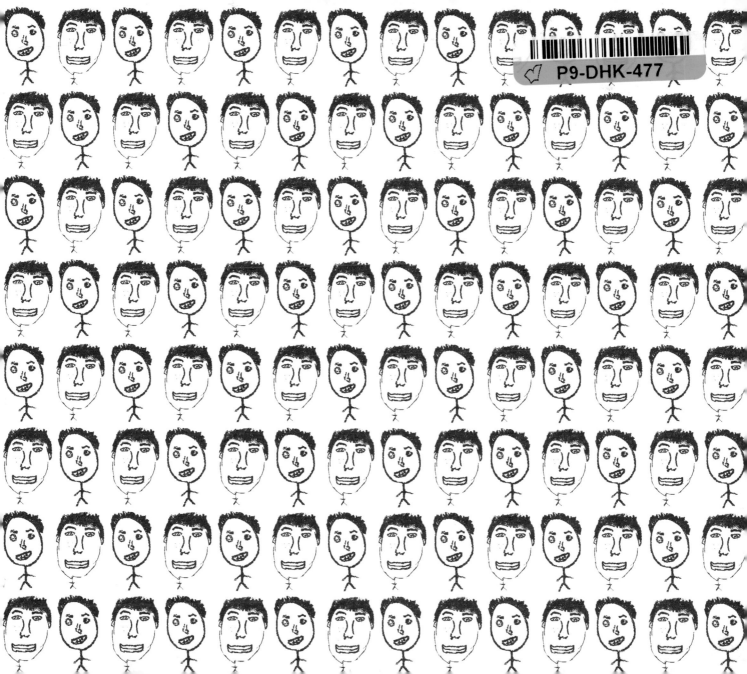

THE BATALI BROTHERS COOKBOOK

THE BATALI BROTHERS COOKBOOK

WITH ADDITIONAL RECIPES FOR THE WHOLE FAMILY FROM MARIO BATALI

BENNO AND LEO BATALI

WITH PHOTOGRAPHS BY SUSI CAHN

ecco

An Imprint of HarperCollinsPublishers

HarperCollins books may be purchased for educational, business, or sales promotional use. For information please write: Special Markets Department, HarperCollins Publishers, 10 East 53rd Street, New York, NY 10022.

FIRST EDITION

Library of Congress Cataloging-in-Publication Data has been applied for.

ISBN 978-0-06-226934-8

13 14 15 16 17   OV/RRD   10 9 8 7 6 5 4 3 2 1

This book is dedicated to our dad on the occasion of his fiftieth birthday

acknowledgments

We would like to thank all the people below for their support and for making this book possible:

Daddy—we love you so much. If it weren't for your inspiring aura we would never be doing this—we would probably not even be here today.

Mommy—we also love you a lot. You were a key piece in making this book possible and you take some really great pictures.

Lisa, our favorite and loving cousin, who first made this book an actual book—you are always there to help us.

And last but not least, the Conger and Jameson families, who helped us eat these delicious meals—without you guys, our table would have been so lonely.

contents

MARIO'S FAMILY FAVORITES

preface

Every year for the last ten years my wife, Susi; our two boys, Benno and Leo; and I have spent the month of August happily lazing through the waning days of summer at our home on Lake Michigan. In 2010, I had to head back to New York City early to put the finishing touches on Eataly for a September 1st open, so I was not around. I would get a call almost daily from one of the boys with a question about a recipe, an ingredient, or a cooking time, and I thought nothing of it, assuming they were simply taking over the kitchen responsibilities in my absence.

On my fiftieth birthday they presented me with a book of those recipes. Of course I'd expected to see my children blossom into fine young men, but it is an indescribable joy to witness this actually taking place. And they continue to exceed Susi's and my expectations daily. When I first opened my surprise gift of recipes I was (and I still am) overcome by the magnificent joy of being a dad. *The Batali Brothers Cookbook* is a labor of love and also of responsibility, totally about our family fascination with hospitality and the pleasure of giving.

I've included some of my own favorite recipes that I prepared for my family when the boys were growing up—which perhaps influenced and set the stage for the book you now hold in your hands. But aside from those recipes—appended at the end of this collection—the dishes and the text within are completely the boys' own and represent cooking on a basic yet thoughtful level.

I am extremely happy to eat when my boys cook and will happily wash the dishes in exchange for a seat at the table when they do. It's hard not to get sentimental when I think about my boys in the kitchen and their badass coolness, so I'm stopping here.

I hope you enjoy this as much as I have.

—Mario Batali

introduction

For our dad's fiftieth birthday we wanted to do something very special, something that would show him that we had paid attention during our times in the kitchen together. We decided to make a cookbook. This cookbook represents what he taught us about food and how to handle it from beginning to end.

Since we were little we have spent a lot of time in the kitchen with our dad. He has taught us to be confident and to try different things. We remember the first time we made scrambled eggs on our own—he was so happy and proud. Sometimes he gets really impatient and yells; other times he can be welcoming and charming. No matter which mood he's in, we always have fun in the end and have a great meal.

Our dad is really special to us. We humor him, love him, and we will never let him down. He is our role model and we always look up to him. He has inspired us so much that we want to follow in his footsteps and be great chefs. This book is basically a thank-you for all he has done for us and all the time he has spent with us.

HE IS THE BEST DAD IN THE WORLD.

SO, DAD . . . HAPPY 50TH BIRTHDAY! WE LOVE YOU.

xxx Benno & Leo

PART ONE

BENNO AND LEO

Cinnamon Swirl French Toast

This is our favorite breakfast dish to eat on the weekend because it reminds us that we should be relaxing and doing what we want. When we were younger we used to eat it every weekend but now we only have it on special occasions, so it is a real treat for us.

Makes 10 slices of French toast

3 eggs
1 cup whole milk
2 teaspoons ground
  cinnamon
2 teaspoons vanilla extract
½ teaspoon ground nutmeg
10 slices cinnamon bread
4 tablespoons (½ stick)
  unsalted butter, plus
  more as needed
Maple syrup and butter,
  for serving

1. In a bowl, beat together the eggs, milk, cinnamon, vanilla extract, and nutmeg.
2. Set a cast-iron or nonstick sauté pan over medium heat.
3. Put a couple of slices of bread in the mix. Coat each side of the bread and let it sit for half a minute to soak up the egg.
4. Put 1 tablespoon of the butter in the pan and let it melt. Put the bread into the pan and cook for 3 minutes on each side or until browned and cooked to your liking.
5. Cook the rest of the bread the same way, adding butter to the pan each time.
6. Serve hot, with maple syrup and butter.

Brown Sugar Pancakes

Brown sugar pancakes are a new recipe that we just tried out, and they turned out AMAZING.
Put these pancakes on your breakfast table and the crowd will go wild.

Serves 6 people
(makes 12 to 14 medium
pancakes)

2 cups all-purpose flour
1 tablespoon baking
   powder
1 pinch salt
1 tablespoon granulated
   sugar
2 eggs
2 cups whole milk
½ teaspoon vanilla extract
2 tablespoons unsalted
   butter, melted, plus
   unmelted butter for
   the pan
3 tablespoons light brown
   sugar
Maple syrup and butter,
   for serving

1. Put a nonstick or cast-iron frying pan on the stove over medium heat.
2. In a medium bowl, mix the flour, baking powder, salt, and granulated sugar together.
3. In a large bowl, beat the eggs with the milk. Add the vanilla extract and the melted butter, then whisk some more.
4. Add the dry ingredients into the wet ingredients in thirds, and whisk. Make sure to get all the lumps out of the batter.
5. When you are done whisking the batter, crumble 2 tablespoons of the brown sugar on top and then stir them in.
6. Take some unmelted butter and heat it in the pan so it melts and bubbles.
7. Then cook in batches: Pour the batter onto the pan (not all of it, just a ladleful at a time—we like a 2- or 3-ounce ladle) so you form good round circles. Flip the pancakes when bubbles form on the top, and cook them till they are ready.
8. Sprinkle the remaining tablespoon of brown sugar over the top and serve hot, with maple syrup and butter.

Scrambled Eggs

Scrambled eggs was the first dish we ever learned how to make. It is simple, delicious, and fun to experiment with. This dish is easy to master and great to teach to your kids.

Serves 4 people

8 eggs
4 tablespoons half-and-half
1 big pinch salt
1 twist cracked black
   pepper
2 tablespoons extra virgin
   olive oil

1. Set a nonstick frying pan on medium heat.
2. Crack all the eggs into a bowl.
3. Take a fork and beat the eggs until they're completely mixed together.
4. Then add the half-and-half, salt, and pepper and beat some more.
5. Add the oil to the pan and swirl it around. Pour the eggs into the pan and let them sit until you see a crust of cooked egg around the outside edge. When you see that crust, take a rubber spatula and push the cooked egg across the pan.
6. Keep doing that until all of the liquid egg has been cooked. This will take about 3 to 5 minutes.
7. Put the egg onto plates and serve.

Kale Salad with Lemon Dressing

We learned how to make this salad this year, and it is delicious. We like to eat it on a summer night because it's light and great to share with others. This recipe will teach people what they can do with their kale.

Serves 8 to 10 people

3 bunches (about 1 pound)
  cavolo nero kale (black
  cabbage or dinosaur
  kale), stemmed
¾ cup pine nuts
1 cup dried currants
1 recipe Lemon Dressing
  (see below)
Salt and ground black
  pepper

LEMON DRESSING
2 lemons
2 tablespoons Dijon
  mustard
1 cup olive oil

1. Slice the kale up into very thin strips.
2. Then take all of the kale and rinse it. Put it in a salad spinner and spin till all the water is out.
3. Put the kale in a salad bowl, and add the pine nuts and the currants.
4. Let sit with a wet paper towel over it.
5. Dress the kale with the Lemon Dressing. Season with salt and pepper to taste.

TO MAKE THE LEMON DRESSING
1. Zest the lemons with a grater like a Microplane, and put the zest in something with a lid—a container that you can shake, like a jar.
2. Roll the lemons on the counter, pressing on them so they have a lot of juice. Then cut the lemons in half and juice them, making sure that there are no seeds. (You should get about ½ cup of juice. If not, juice another lemon.) When you have all the juice, pour it into the jar with the zest.
3. Put the mustard in with the lemon zest and juice.
4. Then add the olive oil.
5. When you are done, shake it all together until it is well mixed.

Triple P Salad

(Potatoes, Peas, and Pesto)

This dish is potato heaven. We love to serve this in the summer because all of the ingredients taste fresh, light, and relaxing.

Serves 8 to 10 people

3 cups peas (freshly
   shucked or frozen)
2¾ pounds mixed potatoes
   (such as purple Peruvian
   and fingerling)
¼ cup extra virgin olive oil
3 big pinches salt, plus
   more to taste
½ cup pesto
1 twist cracked black
   pepper

1. Bring a pot of salted water to a boil. Cook the peas in the boiling water for 2 to 3 minutes.
2. When the peas are done, use a slotted spoon to put them in a bath of ice water, and let them sit for 2 minutes. Drain the peas (reserving the ice water) and add them to your serving bowl.
3. Meanwhile, cut the potatoes in half (or same-sized pieces) and put them in the same pot of boiling water. Bring back up to a boil and cook for 4 to 5 minutes or until cooked through.
4. When the potatoes are done, drain them and put them in the bowl of ice water. Let them sit for 2 minutes. Then take the potatoes out of the water and put them in your serving bowl with the peas.
5. Add the olive oil and salt, and toss.
6. When you are done tossing, add the pesto and then toss some more. Season with more salt and the twist of cracked pepper.

Caprese

The caprese is a very traditional Italian meal that is amazing and easy to make. We like to eat it on a summer day because it's so refreshing. And people will love you when you make it for them.

Serves 6 to 8 people

2 balls fresh mozzarella
   (1 pound each)
3 heirloom tomatoes (about
   2½ pounds total)
1 bunch fresh basil, leaves
   picked (about 21 leaves)
1 drizzle balsamic vinegar
1 drizzle extra virgin olive
   oil
1 pinch salt

1. Cut the mozzarella and the tomatoes into thin slices.
2. Start to lay the tomatoes, mozzarella, and basil leaves on a large plate, making a pattern, and keep that going till you're done.
3. Then when you're done, drizzle the vinegar and olive oil over everything, and sprinkle the salt on top.

Italian Corn

This corn is unforgettable, it is so good. We love to eat it in the summer because that's when it's corn season. If you are having a sale to raise money on your street, we recommend you bring out a grill and do this recipe since it's so simple.

Serves 6 people

6 ears corn
Extra virgin olive oil, for
    drizzling
1 cup balsamic vinegar
    (enough to fill a not-so-
    deep dish)
2 cups Parmigiano-
    Reggiano

1. Preheat the grill to high heat.
2. Shuck all the corn.
3. Drizzle the corn with olive oil and put it on the grill.
4. Turn the corn every 3 minutes to make sure it gets cooked on every side.
5. Pour your balsamic into a shallow bowl or dish, and in another bowl, do the same with the cheese.
6. Then take the corn off the grill and roll it through the balsamic, then the cheese (so the cheese sticks). Do that with every ear.
7. When you are done with that, drizzle a little balsamic and sprinkle a little cheese on all the corn.

Sloppy Sloppy Joes

This is one of the first dishes we learned to make without our dad, which made us feel pretty good. This dish is practically made for a family meal, so you can eat, share, and have fun with very sloppy Sloppy Joes.

Serves 4 to 6 people

2 tablespoons vegetable oil
1½ pounds ground chuck
5 tablespoons tomato paste
2 tablespoons sugar
One 12-ounce jar of mild
  salsa
6 hamburger buns

1. Place a frying pan over medium-high heat. Add the oil and rub it onto the bottom of the pan with a paper towel and tongs.
2. Add the ground beef, and while it's cooking, break it up with something like the back of a spoon. Cook for 3 to 4 minutes.
3. Add the remaining ingredients except for the buns, and mix while still chopping the mixture up with the spoon.
4. When the liquids start to simmer, reduce the heat to low and cook for 4 minutes.
5. Then open the buns and stuff in the meat.

Meatballs

You can't go wrong with meatballs. They go with every occasion and are always delicious. Though the best meatballs are in Italy, these will come very close. Serve them with a nice kale salad (see page 8) and you will have heaven in your mouth.

*Serves 10 people
(makes 30 meatballs)*

1 pound ground chuck
1 pound ground turkey
1 pound ground veal
1 pound ground sausage,
　removed from the casing
2 cups panko breadcrumbs
1 cup grated Parmigiano-
　Reggiano
2 eggs, beaten
½ cup whole milk
½ bunch fresh parsley,
　chopped fine (about
　¼ cup)
1 teaspoon salt
1 teaspoon ground black
　pepper
Three 18-ounce jars of
　your favorite tomato
　sauce, like our dad's

1. Preheat the oven to 400°F.
2. In a large bowl, use your hands to mix the chuck, turkey, veal, sausage, panko, Parmigiano, eggs, milk, parsley, salt, and pepper.
3. When everything is mixed, you can start rolling meatballs: they should be 1 to 2 inches in diameter.
4. When you have rolled the meatballs, place them an inch apart in a nonstick baking pan or on an oiled cookie sheet.
5. Put pan in the oven and bake for 20 minutes.
6. While the meatballs are in the oven, put the tomato sauce in a large pot and heat it until it simmers.
7. When the meatballs are done, use a spatula to remove them from the pan and put them into the sauce.
8. Put a lid on the pot and let it simmer for 10 minutes.
9. To serve, you can transfer the meatballs to a different bowl or just use the pot.

Whole Roasted Chicken on the Grill

Chicken is one of our favorite meats because it is easy to cook and tastes delicious. It is also one of our mother's favorite meals, so we have to like it. We like to serve it with green beans and the Triple P Salad (see page 10).

Serves 4 people

1½ cups pickle juice
3 tablespoons salt, plus
   more to taste
1 whole chicken
8 garlic cloves, peeled
1 lemon, sliced into
   ⅓-inch slices
2 celery stalks
½ onion, peeled and sliced
   into ⅓-inch slices
3 cinnamon sticks
2 tablespoons whole cloves
2 tablespoons whole black
   peppercorns
1 tablespoon dried juniper
   berries
1 tablespoon coriander
   seeds

1. In a bowl large enough to fit the chicken, mix together 6 cups of water, the pickle juice, and the 3 tablespoons of salt. Place the chicken in this brine. It should be covered up to its back, but not completely covered. Refrigerate for at least 2 hours and up to 6.
2. When you are ready to cook the chicken, preheat the grill to high on one side and low on the other. Put a piastra (a flat griddle stone) or a cast-iron pan on the side with the low heat.
3. Remove the chicken from the brine and stuff it with the garlic and half of the lemon slices.
4. Create two trays out of doubled-up aluminum foil: one that will fit the chicken, and one that is smaller.
5. In the larger tray, layer what's left of the sliced lemon along with the celery and the sliced onion, so that the chicken will not touch the foil when it's placed on top.
6. In the smaller tray, put the cinnamon, cloves, peppercorns, juniper berries, and coriander seeds.
7. When the grill is preheated, put the smaller tray on the side that is at high heat (this will add a smoky flavor). Put the larger tray—the one with the vegetables—on the piastra, and then put the chicken on the layer of vegetables. Season the chicken with a sprinkling of salt. Cover the grill.
8. Let cook without opening the lid for 1 hour and 10 minutes or until a thermometer reads 160°F (or until cooked to your liking). Enjoy.

Beef Tacos

These tacos are the tacos you dream about having in Mexico. Take a bite, close your eyes, and enjoy the ride.

*Serves 4 hungry people
(makes 14 to 16 tacos)*

2 tablespoons extra virgin
   olive oil
½ red onion, peeled, cut in
   half, and sliced into thin
   half-moons
2¼ pounds ground chuck
2 teaspoons salt
1½ tablespoons ground
   cumin
1 tube tomato paste (about
   4½ ounces)
4 garlic cloves, peeled:
   3 chopped, 1 left whole
14 to 16 corn tortillas
2 limes
1 bunch (about ½ cup)
   fresh cilantro, leaves
   picked

1. Take a large frying pan, put it over medium-high heat, and let it heat up. Then take the olive oil and drizzle it onto the pan. Add the red onion and let that cook till the onions turn just a tiny bit brown, about 3 to 4 minutes.
2. Add the meat in thirds: add one-third, wait 5 seconds, add the second, wait 5 seconds, and so on. Season with the salt. Then take a wooden stirrer with a sharp edge and chop the meat so it's separated into little parts. Keep doing that and turning the meat so it gets browned and cooked through, about 6 to 8 minutes. Drain some of the grease with a spoon and discard it. But keep some—it adds flavor!
3. When the meat is almost ready, spread the cumin and tomato paste over the meat and stir to mix well. The tomato paste may look disgusting but it makes your tacos less dry, and keeps them wet and delicious.
4. Add the chopped garlic, plus the whole clove (just remember to remove it before serving). That clove will always keep adding flavor to the meat. Cook for about 1 to 2 minutes. Remove the pan from the heat.
5. To cook the tortillas, put the burner on medium-low and throw a tortilla right on the burner. Flip the tortilla with tongs when it is ready. Wrap the cooked tortillas in a towel.
6. To serve, put the meat in a bowl and the tortillas on a plate or in a tortilla holder. Then cut the limes into wedges and put the cilantro leaves in a cup.
7. To make a taco, take a tortilla and put in the meat with some cilantro on top, then squeeze the lime on the meat and enjoy.

Blue Cheese Pocket Burgers

This is a meal that we enjoy on a weekend when we feel very lazy. We love it because it is very easy to make and tastes really good. And you can stuff your pocket burger with anything you want (see the variations below). Also it is very easy to clean up because you can serve it on paper plates.

Serves 4 people

2 teaspoons ground cumin
2 teaspoons ground black pepper
1 teaspoon salt
1¾ pounds ground chuck
½ cup crumbled blue cheese
4 hamburger buns, toasted

VARIATIONS
Blue Cheese Bacon Pocket Burgers
Cheddar Pocket Burgers
Cheddar Bacon Pocket Burgers
Swiss Mushroom Pocket Burgers
Grilled Onion and Mushroom Pocket Burgers

1. Preheat a grill to high heat.
2. Combine the cumin, pepper, and salt in a small bowl.
3. Form your ground chuck into 8 evenly sized thin patties.
4. On one side of each patty, sprinkle a heaping ¼ teaspoon of the cumin mixture (or more to your liking).
5. Flip over 4 of the patties. Making sure that the spices are on the outside of the patty, put a quarter of the blue cheese on the center of each patty (the nonspiced side). These are the bottom patties.
6. Take one of the remaining patties and place it over the blue cheese on one of the bottom patties, making sure that the spices are on the outside. Do this with the remaining 3 patties.
7. Gently push the top patty down around the blue cheese and pinch the sides of the patties together until the burgers are completely sealed around the cheese.
8. Put your burgers on the grill and let them cook for 4 minutes on each side for medium, or until cooked to your liking.
9. To eat a burger, put it on a toasted hamburger bun and enjoy.

Homemade Pasta

Everybody loves pasta, and when you make it yourself, everybody loves it even more. This is a recipe that we always make with our dad when we have a large party because it is fun for everybody to participate in the preparation. We would guarantee that if everyone in the world ate pasta for a day, there would be peace. Like our dad says, there's peace through pasta. When the pasta is cooked, serve it with any variety of the delicious Mario Batali pasta sauces (available at your local market).

Serves 7 people
(makes 1½ pounds fresh pasta)

3½ cups all-purpose flour
5 large eggs
Cornmeal, for the baking
    sheet

1. On your working area, make a large mound of the flour.
2. Punch into the center of the mound until you have the flour shaped like a well. Crack each egg into the well, and with a fork slowly beat only the eggs.
3. Gradually start incorporating the flour into the eggs.
4. When you are three-quarters of the way done, you can use your hands and start to knead the dough. As you do this, everything should start to come together.
5. If the dough is dry, add a touch of water, and if the dough is wet, add a touch of flour.
6. When the dough is completely kneaded, put it in a plastic bag and let it sit at room temperature for 30 minutes.
7. Now you can choose to put your dough through a pasta roller or to flatten it by hand with a rolling pin. Cut your rolled-out pasta into any shape or form.
8. Sprinkle cornmeal over a baking sheet, and spread the pasta out on the cornmeal. Refrigerate for 30 minutes.
9. To cook the pasta, bring a large pot of water to a boil, add a heavy pinch of salt, and cook the pasta for 4 minutes.

MARIO BATALI

PASTA SAUCE

ALLA VODKA

Crafted from Imported San Marzano
Tomatoes & Parmigiano-Reggiano Cheese

Net Wt. 24 oz. (680g)

PRODUCED IN A GREEN FACILITY

Blackberry and Peach Cobbler

This dish is like summer on a plate. This is because these fruits are in season only during the summer. We recommend that to make this you use only local fruits because otherwise it takes away from the final product. Enjoy this with some friends during the sunset and you will be in heaven.

Serves 4 people

4 fresh peaches, peeled, pitted, and sliced
Two 6-ounce containers fresh blackberries
¼ cup granulated sugar
1 cup old-fashioned rolled oats
½ cup light brown sugar, loosely packed
1 pinch salt
6 tablespoons (¾ stick) unsalted butter, cold, cut into cubes
Ice cream, for serving

1. Preheat the oven to 375°F.
2. Put the peaches and blackberries into a bowl, and mix with the granulated sugar. Set aside.
3. In a food processor, put the oats, brown sugar, salt, and butter, and pulse till the mixture has a crumbly texture.
4. Place the fruit in a 6½ x 8-inch baking dish, and then crumble the oat mixture over it until you have an even layer over all the fruit.
5. Bake in the oven for 20 to 30 minutes or until the crust is golden brown and the fruit is bubbling.
6. Let sit for 10 minutes, and then serve warm with ice cream.

Vanilla Cupcakes
(with Buttercream Frosting)

These cupcakes are one of our favorite desserts to share with groups of people. They are great for parties and picnics. They are a wonderful way to end a meal, and kids go crazy over them and will definitely come back asking for more.

Makes 12 cupcakes

8 tablespoons (1 stick) unsalted butter, at room temperature, cut into pieces
1 cup sugar
4 egg whites
1¼ cups self-rising flour
½ cup whole milk
1½ teaspoons vanilla extract
1½ teaspoons grated orange zest

BUTTERCREAM FROSTING
2 cups confectioners' sugar
4½ tablespoons unsalted butter, at room temperature
½ teaspoon vanilla extract
¼ teaspoon salt
3 tablespoons whole milk

1. Preheat the oven to 350°F.
2. Insert cupcake liners into a 12-cupcake tin.
3. Put the butter in the bowl of a standing electric mixer. Use the paddle to cream the butter until smooth.
4. Add the sugar, and cream together until fluffy.
5. Add the egg whites one at a time, beating after each one.
6. Add the flour alternating with the milk, starting with flour and ending with flour.
7. Stir in the vanilla extract and the orange zest, and mix until the batter is smooth.
8. Fill each cupcake liner about three-quarters full with batter.
9. Bake for 25 to 35 minutes, or until a skewer (or cake tester) inserted into the center of a cupcake comes out clean.
10. Let cool completely, then spread the frosting over the tops.

TO MAKE THE BUTTERCREAM FROSTING
1. In the bowl of an electric mixer, beat together the confectioners' sugar, butter, vanilla extract, salt, and milk.
2. If the frosting is too thin to spread, add more confectioners' sugar. If it is too thick, add more milk.

Peach Shortcakes

We discovered this recipe this year and now love it. We like to make this dessert on a summer night when the peaches are so ripe. This dish is really simple and easy to make.

Serves 8 people

1 can (8-pack) Pillsbury
   Grands Flaky Layers
   Buttermilk Biscuits
2 cups whipping cream
2 tablespoons confectioners'
   sugar
2 teaspoons vanilla extract
8 fresh peaches, peeled,
   pitted, and sliced

1. Put a large bowl into the freezer (this will be for the whipped cream).
2. Preheat the oven to 350°F.
3. Separate the biscuits and place them on an ungreased cookie sheet.
4. Bake the biscuits for 14 minutes.
5. At the 12-minute mark, take the bowl from the freezer. Put the whipping cream, confectioners' sugar, and vanilla extract in the bowl and beat with a hand-held electric mixer until whipped.
6. Take out the biscuits and cut them in half. Pile on the peaches and whipped cream.

Daddy's Birthday Cake

(aka Franny's Sunshine Cake)

Our mom makes this cake every year for Dad's birthday. The tradition is that she always makes a mistake and that the cake is never perfect. Though she always messes up, it always tastes good and this is a great recipe. You'll need a 9-inch angel food cake pan for this cake.

Serves 12 to 14 people

8 eggs, separated
1 teaspoon cream of tartar
1⅓ cups sugar
¼ teaspoon salt
½ cup orange juice
1 cup plus 2 tablespoons
  sifted cake flour
1 teaspoon vanilla extract
1 teaspoon almond extract
1 recipe Orange Filling
  (page 36)
1 can mandarin orange
  slices, drained
1 quart fresh berries, sliced
1 recipe Topping (page 36)

1. Preheat the oven to 350°F.
2. In a standing electric mixer, use the whisk attachment to whip the egg whites with the cream of tartar. When they start to double in size, slowly add in ⅔ cup of the sugar. Whip until you have stiff peaks. Set aside.
3. In a large mixing bowl, whisk together the egg yolks, salt, and the remaining ⅔ cup sugar. Gradually add the orange juice and continue to beat until light and fluffy.
4. Combine the two mixtures: Spoon a little whipped egg whites into the yolks and stir. Then fold the rest of the whites into the mixture in two additions.
5. Deftly fold in the flour, vanilla extract, and almond extract.
6. Pour the batter into an ungreased 9-inch angel food cake pan and bake for 35 to 40 minutes or until a cake tester comes out clean.
7. Remove the pan from the oven and place it upside down. Leave it like that until the cake is cool.
8. Once it has cooled, run a sharp knife around the edge of the cake to separate it from the pan. Invert the pan over a serving plate, and let gravity do its thing.
9. Carefully cut the cake in half horizontally with a large serrated knife.

ORANGE FILLING

¾ cup sugar

1 egg

2½ tablespoons all-
purpose flour

Juice and grated zest of
1 orange

2 cups heavy cream

TOPPING

Unsalted butter, for
greasing the foil

½ cup sugar

1 cup sliced almonds

10. Frost the top of the bottom half with some of the orange filling, and then layer some of the mandarin orange slices and berries on top of the frosting.
11. Place the top half over the bottom half, and then frost the top and sides of the cake with the remaining orange filling. Place the remaining mandarin oranges and berries on top of the cake.
12. Sprinkle the topping over the cake and enjoy.

TO MAKE THE ORANGE FILLING

1. Combine the sugar, egg, flour, orange juice, and orange zest in a double boiler and cook over simmering water until thick, about 5 to 8 minutes. Cool to room temperature.
2. Whip the cream till almost stiff. Fold in the cooled orange mixture. Whisk until you have stiff peaks.

TO MAKE THE TOPPING

1. Butter a piece of aluminum foil.
2. In a heavy skillet over high heat, cook the sugar until it is caramelized (turns a medium brown color). Swirl the pan carefully to get all of the sugar to caramelize evenly.
3. Pour the sliced almonds over the caramelized sugar and stir with a wooden spoon to coat the almonds. Spread the almonds out on the piece of buttered foil, and let them cool.
4. When they are cool, crush or chop the nuts.

MARIO'S FAMILY FAVORITES

Carrots in Scapece with Cumin and Honey

Cooked carrots were never a hit in our house till sweet honey and exotic cumin hit the luscious orange heroes. Now the boys actually request them as a side dish, especially in the late fall when carrots are at their sweetest.

Serves 8 to 10 as a side dish

Salt
10 medium to large
   carrots, cut into
   ½-inch-thick coins
½ cup red wine vinegar
1 garlic clove, finely
   minced
½ cup extra virgin olive
   oil
3 tablespoons honey
1 tablespoon cumin
   seeds, toasted

Bring 8 quarts of water to a boil in a pasta pot, and when it is boiling, add 2 tablespoons of salt. Add the carrots and boil until just tender, 5 to 6 minutes.

Meanwhile, combine the vinegar, garlic, oil, honey, cumin, and salt to taste in a bowl.

Drain the carrots and transfer them to a bowl. Add the sauce to the warm carrots and toss until well mixed. Cover the bowl with plastic wrap and refrigerate for several hours or overnight.

Remove the bowl from the fridge 30 minutes before serving, to allow the carrots to come to room temperature.

Spring Onion Frittelle

These easy little scallion pancakes take less than 10 minutes to make, and the batter is a superdelicious vehicle for any small bits of leftover vegetables from the night before. Simply substitute 1 cup of anything you have for the sliced scallions.

Serves 8 to 10 as a side dish

4 large eggs
1 cup all-purpose flour
2 tablespoons baking
  powder
1 cup seltzer water,
  chilled
½ cup freshly grated
  Parmigiano-Reggiano
Salt and freshly ground
  black pepper, to taste
4 bunches spring onions
  or scallions, whites
  and about 2 inches of
  greens sliced
2 tablespoons extra
  virgin olive oil

In a medium-sized bowl, combine the eggs, flour, baking powder, seltzer water, cheese, and a pinch each of salt and pepper. Whisk well to combine. Cover, and let rest in the fridge for at least 20 minutes.

Remove the batter from the fridge, and stir in the spring onions.

In a 12- to 14-inch nonstick or cast-iron skillet, heat the olive oil over medium-high heat. Drop tablespoons of the batter into the hot skillet to make 2-inch pancakes. Cook until golden brown on the first side, then flip to brown on the other side. As they are cooked, use a slotted spoon to transfer the frittelle to a plate lined with paper towels to drain.

Sprinkle with salt to taste, and serve immediately.

Oven-Dried Cherry Tomatoes with Breadcrumbs

These are much, much better than any commercially available sun-dried tomatoes—and so easy to make that the kids will be clamoring not only to eat them, but to make them as well.

Makes about 3 quarts

4 pounds cherry
tomatoes (Sun Gold is
my favorite variety)
½ cup extra virgin olive
oil
3 tablespoons flaky sea
salt, such as Maldon
2 tablespoons freshly
ground black pepper
1 cup fresh
breadcrumbs

Preheat the oven to 350°F. Line a heavy baking sheet with parchment paper.

In a large mixing bowl, toss the tomatoes with the oil, sea salt, pepper, and breadcrumbs. Spread the tomatoes out on the baking sheet, and bake for 30 minutes, or until the skins are beginning to shrivel.

Reduce the oven temperature to 250°F and continue baking for 3 hours, or until the tomatoes have collapsed and are slightly wrinkled but still moist. Remove from the oven. Let the tomatoes cool, and see how long they last around the house. I like to serve them with a sprinkling of fresh herbs and a dollop of room-temperature ricotta seasoned with red pepper flakes.

Brussels Sprouts with Pecorino and Thyme

Blanching the Brussels sprouts for 3 minutes leaves the kitchen less smelly and helps them retain a crunchiness that makes them more delicious. Adding cheese is almost like cheating, as doing so instantly transforms the sprouts into a virtual fondue.

Serves 8 to 10 as a side dish

Salt

2 pounds Brussels
sprouts, any tough or
discolored outer leaves
removed

¼ cup extra virgin olive
oil

2 teaspoons finely
chopped fresh thyme
leaves

4 ounces Pecorino
Romano, cut into
¼-inch cubes as best
you can

Freshly ground black
pepper, to taste

Bring 8 quarts of water to a boil in a pasta pot. Set up an ice bath nearby.

When the water comes to a boil, add 2 tablespoons of salt. Drop the Brussels sprouts into the boiling water, and when the water returns to the boil, cook for 3 minutes. Then drain the Brussels sprouts and plunge them into the ice bath. Once they have cooled, drain, trim off the tough ends, and cut them in half lengthwise.

In a 14-inch sauté pan, heat the oil over medium heat. Add the thyme leaves and cook until they are crispy, 2 to 3 minutes. Carefully add the Brussels sprouts to the pan (they will cause a spattering ruckus), and cook over medium heat until they are tender and starting to brown, 7 to 10 minutes.

Add the Pecorino cubes and cook, stirring gently, until the cheese starts to melt around the edges, about 3 minutes. Season with black pepper and serve immediately.

Fregula with Corn

As a family, there's nothing on the Otto menu that we look forward to more than this simple pasta and corn antipasto. It captures the sweet end of summer sun and locks it into every bite. This antipasto might easily become the only side dish for anything you throw on the grill from August to October.

Serves 6

Kosher salt
½ pound (about 1⅓
  cups) fregula
1 tablespoon extra
  virgin olive oil
1 cup fresh corn kernels
Maldon or other flaky
  sea salt
¼ cup thinly sliced
  scallions
2 tablespoons Lemon
  Vinaigrette (see below)
Coarsely ground black
  pepper

LEMON VINAIGRETTE

Makes ¾ cup
4 tablespoons lemon
  juice
½ cup extra virgin olive
  oil

Bring 4 quarts of water to a boil in a large pot and add 2 tablespoons kosher salt. Add the fregula and cook until al dente, 10 to 12 minutes. Drain well.

Meanwhile, heat a large cast-iron or other heavy skillet over high heat until smoking hot. Add the olive oil and heat until very hot, then add the corn and cook, stirring once or twice, until the kernels are charred in spots, about 2 minutes (watch out for popping corn kernels). Season with Maldon salt and cook, stirring, until just tender, another minute or so. Transfer to a large bowl and allow to cool.

Add the fregula and scallions to the corn, then add the vinaigrette and toss well. Season generously with Maldon salt and with pepper. Serve, or let stand at room temperature for 1 hour to bring out the flavors. The fregula can be refrigerated overnight; let it come to room temperature before serving.

To make the lemon vinaigrette: Combine all the ingredients and mix well.

Grilled Mozzarella Sandwiches

This is a jacked-up version of the classic diner grilled cheese, with a rich eggy crust that is crisp yet tender. The star of the show is the mozzarella, so it is worth buying the real thing imported from Italia.

Serves 4

1 pound fresh buffalo
mozzarella, cut into 4
equal pieces about 3
inches by 4 inches
Eight ½-inch-thick
slices firm white
sandwich bread
2 large eggs
½ cup heavy cream
1 teaspoon fresh thyme
leaves
1 teaspoon salt
A grating of nutmeg
¼ cup extra virgin olive
oil
2 tablespoons unsalted
butter

Place the mozzarella on 4 slices of the bread. Cover with the 4 remaining slices to form sandwiches. Trim the crusts off to make perfect 4-inch squares.

In a wide shallow bowl, whisk the eggs. Add the cream, thyme leaves, salt, and nutmeg and whisk until well blended.

In a 10- to 12-inch nonstick sauté pan, heat 2 tablespoons of the olive oil over medium-high heat until smoking. Add 1 tablespoon of the butter and cook until the sizzling subsides. Dip 2 of the sandwiches into the egg mixture, turning to coat, place in the pan, and cook until golden brown on first side, about 2 minutes. Flip over and brown on the other side. Transfer the sandwiches to individual plates and repeat the process with the remaining 2 tablespoons olive oil, 1 tablespoon butter, and 2 sandwiches. Cut in half, and serve immediately.

Leo Pizza (Guanciale)

When we opened Otto, each of us asked our kids what they'd like as their signature pizza. Leo started with tomato and cacio. In a month or so his taste had evolved to this outstanding example of his early antiestablishment ethos.

1 ounce guanciale or pancetta (have the meat sliced ¼ inch thick when you buy it), cut into matchsticks, or 1½ slices good American bacon, cut crosswise into ¼-inch-wide strips
Scant ¼ cup rinsed canned chickpeas
¼ cup Pomì strained tomatoes
1 recipe Pizza Dough (see page 54)
½ cup grated fresh mozzarella
1 tablespoon coarsely chopped fresh Italian parsley

Cook the guanciale in a small sauté pan over medium heat until it has rendered its fat and is golden brown, 8 to 10 minutes. Using a slotted spoon, transfer to paper towels to drain.

Combine the guanciale and chickpeas in a small bowl, mixing well. Spread the tomatoes evenly over the parbaked pizza crust (see page 54), leaving a ½-inch border. Scatter the mozzarella over the sauce, then scatter the chickpeas and guanciale over the top. Broil as directed, then scatter the parsley over the pizza, cut into 4 slices, and serve.

Benno Pizza
(Pesto)

Benno has always been a huge fan of simple delights from Liguria, so it makes sense that his signature pizza is the only one that doesn't include tomato sauce. In the winter, we make a pesto out of broccoli just for fun, and to great success and happiness.

6 tablespoons Basil
   Pesto (see below)
1 recipe Pizza Dough
   (see page 54)
½ cup grated fresh
   mozzarella

BASIL PESTO

Makes 1 cup

3 tablespoons pine nuts
2 cups fresh basil leaves
1 clove garlic, peeled
Pinch of salt
½ cup extra virgin olive
   oil
¼ cup freshly grated
   Parmigiano-Reggiano

Spread the pesto evenly over the parbaked pizza crust (see page 54), leaving a ½-inch border. Scatter the mozzarella over the pesto. Broil as directed, then cut into 4 slices and serve.

To make the basil pesto: Combine the pine nuts, basil, garlic, and salt in a large stone mortar and grind with the pestle until the mixture forms a paste. Slowly drizzle in the olive oil, beating all the while with a wooden spoon. Add the Parmigiano 1 tablespoon at a time, beating until the mixture forms a thick paste. The pesto can also be made in a food processor. The pesto can be stored in a jar, topped with a thin layer of extra virgin olive oil, for several weeks in the refrigerator.

Pizza Dough

Our dough is a little wetter than a standard bread dough, but this style produces the best results with our method of cooking. We use a hot griddle to parcook the pizza crusts, but you can also use a 10-inch enameled cast-iron frying or grilling pan or a smooth cast-iron pancake griddle.

Makes about 2 pounds

1¼ cups warm water
  (95°F)
One ¼-ounce package
  active dry yeast
1½ teaspoons sugar
3½ cups "00" flour
Scant 2 tablespoons salt
¼ cup extra virgin olive
  oil
Semolina for dusting

To make the dough: Whisk the warm water, yeast, and sugar together in a bowl. Let stand in a warm place for 10 minutes, or until the yeast is foamy.

Combine the flour and salt in a large bowl and whisk together. Make a well in the center of the dry ingredients and add the yeast mixture and oil. Using a wooden spoon, stir the wet ingredients into the dry ingredients until the mixture is too stiff to stir, then mix with your hands in the bowl until the dough comes together and pulls away from the sides of the bowl. Turn the dough out onto a lightly floured work surface and knead, adding only as much flour as necessary to prevent sticking, until smooth, elastic, and only slightly sticky. Transfer the dough to a large oiled bowl, turning to coat, cover with a kitchen towel or plastic wrap, and let rise in a warm place for 1 to 1½ hours, until doubled in size.

To shape the dough: Punch down the dough and turn it out onto a well-floured work surface. Divide it into 8 pieces (about 4 ounces each) and shape each one into a ball. Cover with a tea towel and let stand for 15 minutes before stretching the dough. Or, for easier handling, transfer the balls to a floured baking sheet and refrigerate until cold.

To stretch and parbake the dough: Dust a large work surface with a mixture of flour and semolina. If the dough has been refrigerated, transfer one ball to the work surface and let stand just until still cool but not cold (about 60°F if tested with an instant-read thermometer).

Meanwhile, preheat the griddle pan over medium heat until very hot, about 5 minutes.

Using your hands, begin to press and stretch the dough into a 9- to 10-inch round, adding only enough additional flour and semolina to the work surface to keep the dough from sticking; using one hand as a guide, slope a slightly thicker rim all around the circle of dough. Work quickly, and be careful not to overwork the dough; if it resists or shrinks back as you shape it, let it rest briefly before proceeding. (If you prefer, you can roll out the dough with a rolling pin. Lightly flour the work surface and the rolling pin; sprinkle the rolling pin with more flour as necessary to prevent sticking.)

Carefully place the dough round on the preheated griddle pan and cook until barely tan on the first side and browned in a few spots, 2 to 3 minutes. As the crust cooks, if you see any parts that remain undercooked, especially any thicker parts, simply press them against the pan so they cook a bit more; once the dough has set, you can move the crust around as necessary for more even cooking. Flip the crust over and cook until the second side is completely dry, about 1 minute longer.

Transfer the crust to a wire rack or a baking sheet, brushing off any excess flour, and allow to cool. Repeat with the remaining dough. (The parbaked crusts can be refrigerated overnight or frozen, well wrapped, for up to 2 weeks.)

To top each pizza and broil it: Place the parbaked pizza crust on a pizza peel or baking sheet. Spread the tomato sauce evenly over the crust, leaving a ½-inch border all around, and top with any remaining ingredients as specified in the individual recipe. (Do not put the sauce and any other ingredients on the pizza crust until ready to broil it, or the crust may become soggy.)

Slide the pizza under the broiler, about 4 inches from the heat source, and broil for 7 or 8 minutes (or as otherwise noted in the individual recipe), until the topping ingredients are heated and/ or cooked through and the crust is charred and blistered in spots. Watch closely so that the ingredients don't burn, and move the pizza around or lower the broiler rack if necessary. (Sometimes during this stage, depending on the topping, the bottom may start to become soggy; if that happens, you can simply slip the pizza back onto the griddle momentarily to recrisp the crust.)

Finish the pizza with any remaining ingredients, as described in the individual recipe, and cut into slices with a pizza wheel, kitchen shears, or a very sharp knife. Serve hot.

Baked Ziti

Benno's Little Italy favorite, this is a perfect recipe for kids as there is plenty of room for variation on the theme. Sometimes we add chopped salami or leftover roasted vegetables to change it up a bit.

Serves 4

2 tablespoons salt
1 pound ziti
2 cups high-quality
  basic tomato sauce
  (store bought is fine)
2 cups Besciamella
  Sauce (see below)
1 pound fresh buffalo
  mozzarella, cut into
  ½-inch cubes
½ cup freshly grated
  Parmigiano-Reggiano
½ cup fresh
  breadcrumbs

BESCIAMELLA SAUCE

5 tablespoons butter
4 tablespoons flour
3 cups whole milk
2 teaspoons salt
½ teaspoon freshly
  grated nutmeg

Preheat the oven to 425°F.

Bring 6 quarts of water to a boil in a large pot, and add 2 tablespoons of salt. Cook the ziti for 2 minutes short of the package instructions; it should be too al dente to eat. Drain and rinse under cold water until cool. Drain a second time and place in a large bowl.

Add the tomato sauce, besciamella, mozzarella, and Parmigiano to the ziti and stir to mix well. Divide the pasta and sauce mixture among four individual gratin dishes. Sprinkle with the breadcrumbs.

Bake for about 20 minutes, until bubbling and crusty on top. Serve immediately.

To make the besciamella sauce: In a medium saucepan, heat the butter until melted. Add flour and stir until smooth. Over medium heat, cook until light golden brown, about 6 to 7 minutes.

Meanwhile, heat the milk in a separate pan until it's just about to boil. Add the milk to the butter mixture 1 cup at a time, whisking continuously until very smooth and bring to a boil. Cook 30 seconds and remove from the heat. Season with salt and nutmeg and set aside.

Spaghetti with Green Tomato Pesto

Making a pesto with something besides basil is an eye-opener for both adult and younger cooks, and this one is spectacularly delicious. Green tomato pesto is as easy to make as pesto Genovese, and it also helps relieve the pressure of the overflowing garden at the last harvest in October. It will keep well in the freezer for months, so *make a lot* of this!!

Serves 4

2 tablespoons salt, plus
  more for seasoning
¼ cup fresh mint leaves
¼ cup fresh basil leaves
¼ cup fresh Italian
  parsley leaves
¼ cup fresh arugula
  leaves
3 garlic cloves: 1 whole,
  2 chopped
5 green tomatoes, cored
  and roughly chopped
¼ cup plus 2
  tablespoons extra
  virgin olive oil
Salt and freshly ground
  black pepper
1 pound spaghetti
¼ cup freshly grated
  Parmigiano-Reggiano

Bring 6 quarts of water to a boil in a large pot, and add the 2 tablespoons of salt.

Meanwhile, in a food processor, combine the mint, basil, parsley, arugula, whole garlic clove, tomatoes, and the ¼ cup olive oil. Pulse to form a chunky puree. Season aggressively with salt and pepper, and set aside.

In a sauté pan combine the remaining 2 tablespoons olive oil and the chopped garlic, and cook for 2 to 3 minutes. Add 1 cup of the pesto, and set aside.

Cook the spaghetti in the boiling water until just al dente. Drain the pasta and add it to the pan containing the tomato-pesto sauce. Add some of the pasta water to thin the sauce slightly, and toss to coat. Pour into a warmed bowl, sprinkle with the Parmigiano, and serve immediately.

Spaghetti alla Carbonara

The key to this simple dish is to toss and thoroughly mix the cooked pasta with the cheese, eggs, pepper, and pasta water *off the heat* in a warmed bowl, not in the pan. When I serve this in a fancy restaurant, I like to separate the eggs and present the individual egg yolks in nests of pasta, which cooks the yolks and forms an even creamier sauce. Be sure to use the best-quality farm-fresh eggs if you plan on this netless high-wire parlor trick.

Serves 6

Kosher salt
5 ounces sliced
   pancetta, cut into
   ½-inch-wide strips
¼ cup extra virgin olive
   oil
1 tablespoon coarsely
   ground black pepper
6 fresh large eggs
1 pound spaghetti
½ cup freshly grated
   Parmigiano-Reggiano,
   plus extra for serving
¼ cup grated Pecorino
   Romano

Bring 6 quarts of water to a boil in a large pot and add 3 tablespoons of kosher salt.

Meanwhile, combine the pancetta and oil in another large pot and cook over medium-high heat until the pancetta has rendered some of its fat and is lightly browned, about 7 minutes. Stir in the pepper and remove from the heat.

Separate the eggs, being careful to keep the yolks intact, putting the whites in a small bowl and the yolks in a shallow dish.

Drop the pasta into the boiling water and cook until just al dente. Drain, reserving ⅔ cup of the pasta water.

Add the reserved pasta water to the pancetta and bring to a simmer over medium heat. Add the egg whites and cook, whisking furiously, until they are frothy but not set, about 1 minute. Add the pasta, stirring and tossing well to coat. Stir in the cheeses.

Divide the pasta among six bowls, making a nest in the center of each portion. Gently drop an egg yolk into each nest and serve immediately, advising your guests to stir the yolk into the pasta so it will cook. Pass additional grated Parmigiano on the side.

Penne all'Arrabbiata

Just how "angry" *(arrabbiata)* you want your pasta to be is up to you, but one full tablespoon of chili flakes is the real deal at our house. If you have milder palates in your home, then back the chili down to a teaspoon and serve a bowl of angry flakes on the side.

Serves 6

Kosher salt
¼ cup tomato paste
1 tablespoon hot red
   pepper flakes
1½ cups Pomì strained
   tomatoes, simmered
   until reduced by half
1 pound penne
Maldon or other flaky
   sea salt
¼ cup extra virgin olive
   oil
Freshly grated
   Parmigiano-Reggiano
   for serving

Bring 6 quarts of water to a boil in a large pot and add 3 tablespoons of kosher salt.

Meanwhile, combine the tomato paste and pepper flakes in a large pot and stir over low heat just until fragrant. Stir in the tomatoes and remove from the heat.

Drop the pasta into the boiling water and cook until just al dente. Drain the pasta, reserving ¾ cup of the pasta water.

Add the pasta and the reserved pasta water to the tomato sauce and stir and toss over medium heat until the pasta is well coated. Season with salt if necessary, then add the oil, tossing well. Serve immediately, with grated Parmigiano on the side.

Chicken Cooked Under a Brick

Cooking under a common construction item makes this classic Tuscan dish seem more fun and accessible—and it is a great way to demystify crisp skin and juicy fragrant happiness.

Serves 6

2 young chickens
    (about 3 pounds
    each)
3 tablespoons fennel
    pollen or ground
    toasted fennel seeds
¼ cup coarse sea salt
    or kosher salt
1 tablespoon freshly
    ground black
    pepper
1 tablespoon chopped
    fresh thyme
¼ cup extra virgin
    olive oil
About ½ cup chopped
    fresh Italian
    parsley
Lemon wedges for
    serving

Using kitchen shears or a sharp knife, cut down along both sides of the backbone of each chicken and remove it. Turn the chickens skin side up and press down hard on them with your palms to crack the breastbones and flatten them. Remove the excess fat and pat the chickens dry with paper towels.

In a small bowl, mix together the fennel pollen, salt, pepper, and thyme. Pat the mixture onto both sides of the chickens, coating them generously. Wrap each one tightly in plastic wrap, place on a baking sheet or in a baking dish, and refrigerate for 12 hours.

An hour before you are ready to grill, remove the chickens from the refrigerator. Prepare a gas or charcoal grill for indirect grilling. Wrap two clean bricks in a double thickness of heavy-duty aluminum foil and place them on the hot part of the grill to preheat.

Gently blot the chickens dry. Rub the birds all over with the olive oil.

Using pot holders or oven mitts, move the bricks to the side of the grill. Oil the grill rack, using a clean rag dipped in oil or a basting brush. Place the chickens skin side down on the line midway between coals and no coals. Place a brick on top of each chicken, cover the grill, and cook for 10 minutes. Move the bricks to the side of the grill again, carefully lift up each chicken, making sure that the skin doesn't tear (gently slide a thin spatula under the chicken to detach it if necessary), and place skin side up on the hot part of the grill. Place the bricks on top again, cover the grill, and cook for 15 minutes, being careful to snuff any flare-ups with a squirt gun (or, as in my case, a beer).

Remove the bricks, carefully turn the chickens over, and cook, still on the hot part of the grill, for 5 minutes more, or until the thickest part of the thigh registers 165°F. Transfer the chickens to a platter and let rest for 5 to 10 minutes. Sprinkle the chickens with the parsley and serve with lemon wedges.

Chicken Thighs with Saffron, Green Olives, and Mint

Braising is by far the easiest cooking technique to master and is perfect for kids of any age. Do not short the time needed to brown the thighs and create a deep golden-brown crust; it will pay off in spades with the complexity of flavor in the finished dish.

Serves 4

Flour for dredging
12 chicken thighs (2½
  to 3 pounds), rinsed
  and patted dry
Salt and freshly ground
  black pepper
¼ cup extra virgin olive
  oil
2 large red onions,
  thinly sliced
½ teaspoon saffron
  threads
1 cup small green
  olives, pitted
1 medium carrot, finely
  chopped
3 cups chicken stock
½ cup fresh mint leaves

Spread the flour on a plate. Season the chicken thighs liberally with salt and pepper and dredge in the flour. In a Dutch oven, heat the olive oil over high heat until smoking. Add 6 thighs at a time and brown well on all sides. Transfer to a plate.

Add the onions and saffron to the pot and cook until the onions are softened, 8 to 10 minutes. Add the olives, carrot, and stock and bring to a boil. Return the chicken thighs to the pot, arranging them in a single layer, and bring to a boil. Lower the heat to a simmer, cover the pot tightly, and simmer for 15 minutes.

Remove the lid and cook, uncovered, until the chicken is just cooked through, about 10 minutes. Transfer the chicken to a platter. Season the sauce with salt and pepper to taste and add the mint leaves. Pour the sauce over the chicken thighs, and serve.

Sausage with Peppers

One of the most valuable lessons in a cook's life is "know your butcher," and buying great butcher-shop sausage is one of the rewards. We like fennel or anise seeds in our sausage and often buy half hot and half sweet to play a little "Italian roulette" with our chile-fearing friends (the few that exist).

Serves 8

6 tablespoons extra
  virgin olive oil
1 red onion, thinly sliced
5 red bell peppers, cored,
  seeded, and cut into
  ½-inch-wide strips
5 yellow bell peppers,
  cored, seeded, and
  cut into ½-inch-wide
  strips
2 tablespoons hot red
  pepper flakes
2 teaspoons dried
  oregano
One 6-ounce can tomato
  paste
1 cup dry red wine
16 high-quality store-
  bought sausages

In a 10- to 12-inch sauté pan, heat the olive oil over medium heat until smoking. Add the onion, bell peppers, red pepper flakes, and oregano, and cook until the vegetables are softened, 8 to 10 minutes. Add the tomato paste and cook, stirring, until the paste turns a darker color, about 10 minutes. Add the red wine and simmer for 10 minutes. Remove from the heat and allow to cool.

Place a very large skillet over medium heat (use two pans to brown the sausages if necessary, then combine in one pan). Prick the sausages all over and add them to the pan. Cook, turning often, until dark golden brown, 7 to 9 minutes. Add the pepper mixture and bring to a boil. Lower the heat and simmer for 15 minutes, adding water, about ¼ cup at a time, to keep the consistency near that of a ragu.

Divide the sausage and peppers among 8 warmed dinner plates, and serve immediately.

Grilled Lamb Chops

This was Leo's first favorite at Babbo. Lamb chops easily become transcendent when you use a simple dry rub to impart complex flavor. Leo loves the idea of a yogurt sauce and is a huge fan of tzatziki.

Serves 6

Grated zest of 3 lemons
¼ cup coarsely chopped
   fresh mint, plus
   4 whole sprigs for
   garnish
1 tablespoon sugar
Kosher salt and freshly
   ground black pepper
24 lamb rib chops
   (about 3½ pounds)
1 cup goat's-milk
   yogurt, such as Coach
   Farm
1 tablespoon cumin
   seeds, toasted and
   finely ground in a
   spice grinder

Combine two-thirds of the lemon zest (reserve the rest for garnish), the chopped mint, sugar, and 1 teaspoon each salt and pepper in a food processor and process until the mixture has the texture of coarse sand.

Rub each chop well on both sides with a little of the mint mixture. Place on a baking sheet or platter, cover, and set aside at room temperature.

Preheat a gas grill or prepare a fire in a charcoal grill.

Combine the yogurt and cumin in a small bowl, blending well. Season with salt and pepper and transfer to a small serving bowl. Set aside.

Grill the chops, turning once, until medium-rare, about 2 minutes on each side. Pile the chops on a serving platter and garnish with the reserved lemon zest and the mint sprigs. Set out the cumin yogurt next to the platter, and serve immediately.

Lamb Shanks with Leeks and Grapes

In the kitchen, nothing is more satisfying and magical than braising. These shanks are slightly tarted up with the muted sweetness of the leeks and the bright refreshing hit from the grapes.

Serves 8 to 10 as a main course

10 large, meaty lamb
shanks
Salt and freshly ground
black pepper
6 tablespoons olive oil
2 Spanish onions,
chopped into ¼-inch
dice
18 garlic cloves
5 carrots, peeled and cut
into 1-inch pieces
6 leeks, white and light
green parts only,
trimmed, halved
lengthwise, cut
crosswise into thin
half-moons, rinsed
thoroughly, and
drained
2 cups dry white wine
1 cup basic tomato sauce
(for quick results, try
my Mario Batali pasta
sauces by Gia Russa)
3 cups chicken stock
2 cups red grapes

Preheat the oven to 375°F.

Rinse and dry the lamb shanks, and season them liberally with salt and pepper. In a very large heavy-bottomed Dutch oven, heat the olive oil over medium-high heat until smoking. Add the lamb shanks, 5 at a time, and sear until dark golden brown all over, 10 to 12 minutes per batch. Remove the shanks and set them aside.

Add the onions, garlic, carrots, and leeks to the pot and cook until softened, 8 to 10 minutes.

Add the wine, tomato sauce, and stock to the vegetables and bring to a boil. Return the lamb shanks to the pot and bring back to a boil. Cover the pot tightly, place it in the oven, and bake for about 1½ hours, until the meat is fork-tender.

Remove the pot from the oven, check the sauce for seasoning, and then add the grapes. Stir them in gently, and serve directly from the pot.

Rosticciana
(Ribs Italian-Style)

I have never met anyone who can resist this succulent Italian variation on messy, tasty barbecued ribs. You can prep them two days in advance and break them out when a party seems imminent.

Serves 6

¼ cup paprika

3 tablespoons packed
brown sugar

3 tablespoons salt

1 tablespoon ground
cumin

6 garlic cloves, finely
minced

2 cups of your favorite
barbecue sauce

3 large racks baby back
ribs (about 2½ to 3
pounds per rack)

10 bunches rosemary,
soaked overnight in
water to cover

In a small bowl, combine the paprika, brown sugar, salt, cumin, and garlic and mix well. Place the racks on a large baking sheet and rub generously on both sides with the spice mixture. Let stand for 2 hours at cool room temperature, or wrap in plastic and refrigerate for at least 6 hours, or up to 24 hours.

Prepare a gas grill for indirect grilling over low heat. Place a drip pan with an inch or so of water under the cool part of the grill. Pour about ⅔ cup of the barbecue sauce into a small bowl for basting, and pour the rest into a small serving bowl; refrigerate both bowls until about 30 minutes before serving.

Place the ribs on the cooler part of the grill, lay 1 bunch of wet rosemary on the hot part of the grill, and immediately cover the grill. (If your grill isn't large enough to arrange the 3 racks in a single layer for indirect cooking, place 2 of them on the grill and put the third one on top of them.) Cook the ribs for 5 hours; the temperature in the grill should be roughly 250°F. Every 30 minutes, place another bunch of wet rosemary on the hot part of the grill and immediately cover the grill to keep it smoky. Thirty minutes before the ribs are done, brush a light coating of barbecue sauce over them, and then repeat every 10 minutes.

Transfer the racks to a carving board and cut them into individual ribs. Serve with the remaining barbecue sauce.

Lemon Sponge Cake with Pear Marmalade

This is my favorite kind of Italian dessert, one that happily rides the line between after-dinner dessert and traditional Italian mid-afternoon treat. If you don't feel the love for making homemade pear marmalade, use your favorite commercial jam and don't tell anyone.

Serves 6

Unsalted butter, for
greasing the cake
pans
2½ cups cake flour
½ teaspoon salt
2 teaspoons baking
powder
5 tablespoons extra
virgin olive oil
¾ cup granulated sugar
3 large eggs
Grated zest of 6 lemons
½ cup whole milk
¾ cup pear marmalade
Confectioners' sugar, for
garnish

Preheat the oven to 350°F. Butter and flour two 8-inch round cake pans.

In a medium bowl, toss the flour, salt, and baking powder with a fork to mix well.

In a large bowl, beat the olive oil and sugar together with an electric mixer until well blended. Add the eggs one at a time, beating well after each addition. Put the dry ingredients in a sifter and sift about one-third onto the egg mixture. Add the lemon zest and fold in the flour and zest, then stir in about one-third of the milk. Add the remaining flour and milk in two additions each, blending well.

Turn the batter into the prepared cake pans. Bake for 25 minutes, or until the cakes are beginning to pull away from the sides of the pans and spring back when pressed lightly in the center with a finger. Turn the cakes out onto a rack, and invert onto another rack to cool.

To assemble, place one cake layer on a serving plate and spread the marmalade over the top. Place the second layer on top and gently press the layers together. Sprinkle the top of the cake with the confectioners' sugar.

Chocolate Cake from Abruzzo

My grandma Batali was Abruzzese, so this cake always has a special spot in my heart. The boys love it because it literally takes less than an hour to make, from start to cake time.

Serves 8

1½ cups sliced blanched
  almonds
¾ cup sugar
½ cup all-purpose flour
6 tablespoons
  cornstarch
⅛ teaspoon freshly
  grated nutmeg
7 extra-large eggs,
  separated
5 tablespoons unsalted
  butter, melted and
  cooled

GLAZE

6 ounces bittersweet
  chocolate, finely
  chopped
2 tablespoons unsalted
  butter

Preheat the oven to 375°F. Butter a 9-inch round cake pan.

In a food processor, grind the blanched almonds to a fine powder; add a little of the sugar if necessary to keep the nuts from becoming a paste. Set aside.

Sift together the flour, cornstarch, and nutmeg into a small bowl. Set aside.

In a large bowl, beat the egg yolks with an electric mixer until blended. Gradually add the ground almonds and the (remaining) sugar, beating until light and fluffy. Gradually add the flour mixture and then the cooled butter, beating well after each addition.

In another large bowl, beat the egg whites with clean beaters until they form stiff, glossy peaks. Fold them into the batter.

Pour the batter into the prepared cake pan. Bake for about 40 minutes, until the cake is firm to the touch and golden. Let cool in the pan for 15 minutes, then turn out of the pan onto a rack and let cool completely.

To make the glaze: In a small heavy saucepan, melt the chocolate and butter over very low heat, stirring frequently until smooth. Remove from the heat.

Place the cake on a serving plate. Pour the chocolate glaze on top and spread it over the top and sides with a spatula. Serve at room temperature.

Panettone

Christmas morning in our house means panettone for breakfast, and this is a quick, easy, and nonyeast version that you can make with the kids in an hour without any planning. I like to serve this with mascarpone and homemade jam, but cream cheese and jelly will do just fine.

Serves 8

8 tablespoons (1 stick)
 unsalted butter, at
 room temperature
2 large eggs
3 large egg yolks
3½ cups all-purpose
 flour
1 cup whole milk
1 cup sugar
½ cup dried currants,
 soaked in warm
 water for 1 hour and
 drained
Grated zest of 2 oranges
2 teaspoons cream of
 tartar
1½ teaspoons baking
 soda

In the bowl of a stand mixer fitted with the whisk attachment, cream the butter with the eggs and yolks until pale yellow, 3 to 4 minutes. Switch to the dough hook attachment and, with the mixer running, add half of the flour. Add half of the milk and mix for 1 minute. Add the remainder of the flour, followed by the remainder of the milk and then all of the sugar and mix for 20 minutes.

Preheat the oven to 425°F. Butter and flour an 8-inch panettone mold or other deep cake pan, such as a charlotte mold.

Spread the dough out into a rough square on a floured work surface. Sprinkle with the currants, orange zest, cream of tartar, and baking soda and knead for 5 to 10 minutes to incorporate. Place in the prepared pan and bake for 35 to 45 minutes, or until a toothpick inserted in the center comes out dry. The top will be cracked. Unmold the cake onto a rack, then invert and allow to cool. Serve sliced into wedges.

Apple Fritters

A hot, crisp, and delicious fried dessert is the easiest way to impress a crowd, and frying in extra virgin olive oil makes the flavor of these out of this world. . . . Be sure to fill the pot no more than 60 percent full and to fry only three or four fritters at a time to prevent any foam-over.

Serves 4

2 large eggs
¼ cup whole milk
1 cup all-purpose flour
¼ cup sugar
2 tablespoons kirsch
8 cups extra virgin olive
   oil, for deep-frying
6 green apples, such
   as Granny Smith,
   peeled, cored, and
   sliced into ½-inch-
   thick rounds
2 cups vanilla gelato
Cinnamon, for dusting

In a medium bowl, whisk together the eggs and milk. Slowly add the flour, about 3 tablespoons at a time, whisking until incorporated. Stir in the sugar and kirsch. Allow the batter to stand for 10 minutes.

In a large deep pot, heat the olive oil to 375°F. Working in batches of 3 or 4, dip each apple slice into the batter, add to the hot oil, and cook until golden brown. With a slotted spoon, transfer to a paper towel–lined plate to drain.

Place 5 fritters on each of 4 plates, in an overlapping circle. Place a scoop of gelato in the center, sprinkle with cinnamon, and serve.

Strawberry Gelato

The massive difference between homemade and commercial products is never more obvious than with strawberry gelato, or ice cream. The trick in this dish is the condensed milk—it makes the texture of the gelato smoother and more unctuous in a way that will make the gelato machine the most used tool in the kitchen during berry season.

Makes about 5 cups

2 tablespoons nonfat
   dry milk powder
½ cup sugar
1½ cups whole milk
½ cup heavy cream
4 large egg yolks
One 14-ounce can
   sweetened condensed
   milk
1 pound strawberries,
   hulled and chopped
¼ teaspoon salt

Whisk the dry milk and 2 tablespoons of the sugar together in a small bowl. Combine the milk and cream in a large heavy-bottomed saucepan and stir in the dry milk mixture. Bring just to a simmer over medium heat, stirring to dissolve the sugar.

Meanwhile, whisk the egg yolks and 2 tablespoons sugar together in a medium heatproof bowl. Gradually whisk in about 1 cup of the hot milk mixture, then return to the saucepan and stir in the condensed milk. Cook over medium heat, stirring constantly with a heatproof spatula or a wooden spoon, until the custard registers 185°F on an instant-read thermometer.

Strain the custard through a fine-mesh strainer into a heatproof bowl and chill over an ice bath, stirring occasionally, until cold. Cover and refrigerate for at least 6 hours, or, preferably, overnight.

Meanwhile, combine the strawberries, the remaining ¼ cup sugar, and the salt in a medium bowl. Cover and refrigerate for 45 minutes.

Drain the strawberries. Add to the chilled custard, mixing with an immersion blender and breaking up the strawberries. Or transfer the strawberries and custard to a regular blender, in batches, and blend well.

Pour the strawberry mixture into an ice cream maker and freeze according to the manufacturer's instructions. Pack the gelato into a freezer container and freeze for at least 3 hours before serving. The gelato is best served the day it is made.

Macerated Strawberries

The simple step of adding a little sugar and salt to fresh berries can transform them from the delicious to the poetic in half an hour, especially if you are using berries picked at a nearby farm.

Makes about 2⅓ cups

1 pint strawberries,
    preferably small
    berries, washed,
    hulled, and quartered
2 tablespoons sugar, or
    to taste
¼ teaspoon salt

Combine the strawberries, sugar, and salt in a bowl and let stand for 30 minutes.

Taste the berries for sweetness, and add more sugar if necessary before serving.

Tiramisù

This is a perfect recipe for a sophisticated birthday cake for kids or adults. When I make it for kids, I use decaf espresso and skip the liquor.

Serves 6

½ cup strong espresso
(or substitute 2
teaspoons instant
coffee dissolved in ½
cup boiling water),
cooled
¼ cup Italian brandy
2 large eggs, separated
2 large egg yolks
2 tablespoons sugar
2 cups mascarpone
30 small savoiardi
(Italian ladyfingers),
or 15 larger ones,
broken in half
3 ounces bittersweet
chocolate, cut into ¼-
inch pieces
3 ounces milk chocolate,
shaved or grated

In a small bowl, combine the espresso and brandy. Set aside.

In the top of a double boiler, beat the egg yolks and sugar with a hand-held electric mixer until the mixture is pale and thick and forms a ribbon when the beaters are lifted. Transfer to a large bowl and allow to cool for 5 minutes.

In a medium bowl, beat the egg whites to stiff peaks. Fold the mascarpone into the egg yolk mixture one-quarter at a time. Fold in the egg whites and set aside.

Reserve 6 savoiardi, and line six large wine goblets with the remaining savoiardi. Using a pastry brush, paint the cookies with the espresso-brandy mixture. Fill each goblet one-third full with the mascarpone mixture, and sprinkle with the chopped chocolate. Lay 1 of the reserved savoiardi across the center of each and paint with the espresso mixture. Fill the goblets with the remaining mascarpone mixture, and top with the shaved chocolate. Serve at room temperature, or refrigerate and serve chilled.

index

Note: Page references in *italics* indicate photographs.

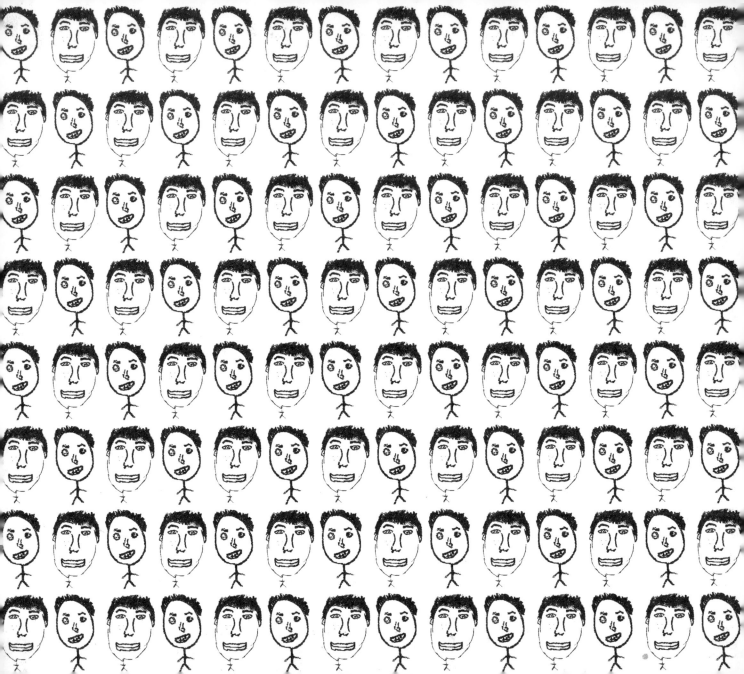